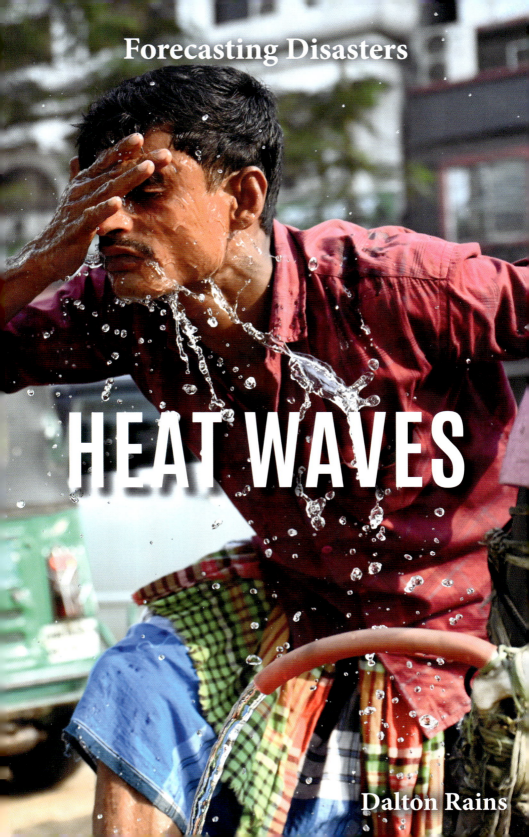

Forecasting Disasters

HEAT WAVES

Dalton Rains

Apex is distributed by North Star Editions:
sales@northstareditions.com | 888-417-0195

Produced for Apex by Red Line Editorial.

Photographs ©: Mamunur Rashid/NurPhoto/AP Images, cover, 1; Monasse T./ANDBZ/Abaca Press/Sipa USA/AP Images, 4–5; Shutterstock Images, 6–7, 8–9, 10–11,12–13, 14–15, 16–17, 18–19, 22–23, 26–27, 30–31, 38–39, 40–41, 42–43, 46–47, 52–53, 54–55, 56–57, 58; National Library of Norway/Flickr, 20–21; Department of Computer Science and Technology/ University of Cambridge, 24–25; Fareed Khan/AP Images, 29; Michael Hanschke/picture-alliance/dpa/AP Images, 32–33; iStockphoto, 34–35; Amanda Diller/NASA, 36–37; Gerard Bottino/SOPA Images/Sipa USA/AP Images, 44–45; Beth A. Keiser/AP Images, 49; Mario Tama/Getty Images News/Getty Images, 50–51

Library of Congress Control Number: 2025930327

ISBN
979-8-89250-661-8 (hardcover)
979-8-89250-696-0 (ebook pdf)
979-8-89250-679-3 (hosted ebook)

Printed in the United States of America
Mankato, MN
082025

NOTE TO PARENTS AND EDUCATORS

Apex books are designed to build literacy skills in striving readers. Exciting, high-interest content attracts and holds readers' attention. The text is carefully leveled to allow students to achieve success quickly.

TABLE OF CONTENTS

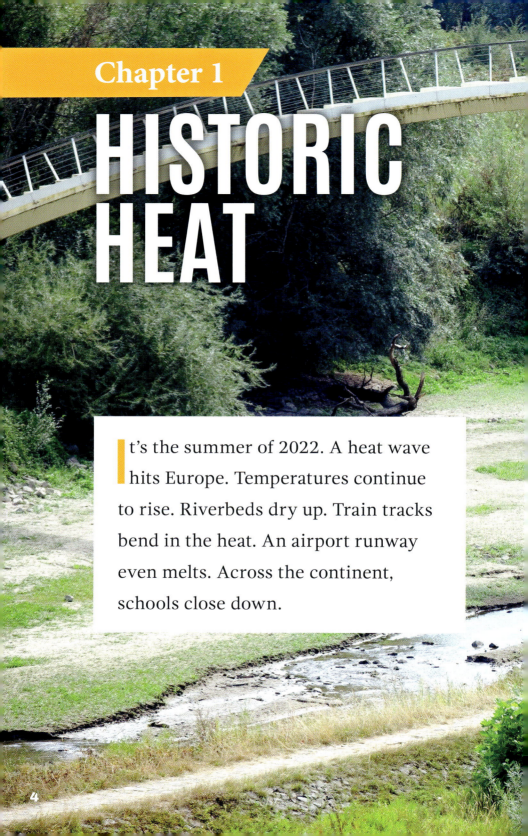

Chapter 1

HISTORIC HEAT

It's the summer of 2022. A heat wave hits Europe. Temperatures continue to rise. Riverbeds dry up. Train tracks bend in the heat. An airport runway even melts. Across the continent, schools close down.

Since the 1980s, Europe has been heating faster than any other continent.

The summer of 2022 was Europe's hottest on record.

Some countries are prepared for the heat. In France, the government works with scientists. Officials watch for severe heat forecasts. Then, they put up posters and ads. They warn people about the heat wave. They remind people to drink water. And they tell people to avoid exercising outdoors.

DEADLY WAVE

A 2003 heat wave killed tens of thousands in Europe. In France alone, 14,000 people died. As a result, governments made plans. They focused on helping people during future heat waves.

In French subway stations, cooling systems can't keep up with the rising temperatures. Officials tell people not to take the trains. People have to work from home. But many houses and apartments don't have air-conditioning. So, French health workers go door to door. They check on people and help treat heatstroke.

CHECKING IN

During heat waves, older people are most at risk of health problems. After the 2003 heat wave, French towns began keeping lists of older people. During heat waves, health workers use the lists. They visit homes and make phone calls. They make sure people are safe.

In 2022, temperatures hit 114.8 degrees Fahrenheit (46°C) in France.

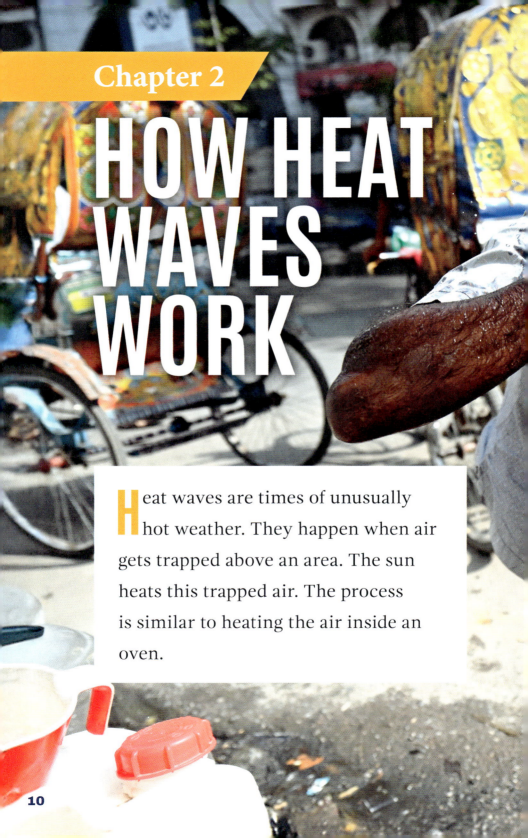

Chapter 2

HOW HEAT WAVES WORK

Heat waves are times of unusually hot weather. They happen when air gets trapped above an area. The sun heats this trapped air. The process is similar to heating the air inside an oven.

Hot weather must last for two or more days to be called a heat wave.

During heat waves, the ground loses moisture. That can leave the soil dry and cracked.

Heat waves are usually caused by high-pressure systems. These systems press air downward. The sinking air acts like a cap. It traps warm air near the ground. The sinking air also pushes out cooler air. It stops clouds from forming. That prevents rain from cooling the air and ground.

GREENHOUSE GASES

Human activities release huge amounts of greenhouse gases. These gases trap heat. They are causing the planet to get warmer. In many places, heat waves are happening more often. The heat waves are getting hotter, too. They also tend to last longer.

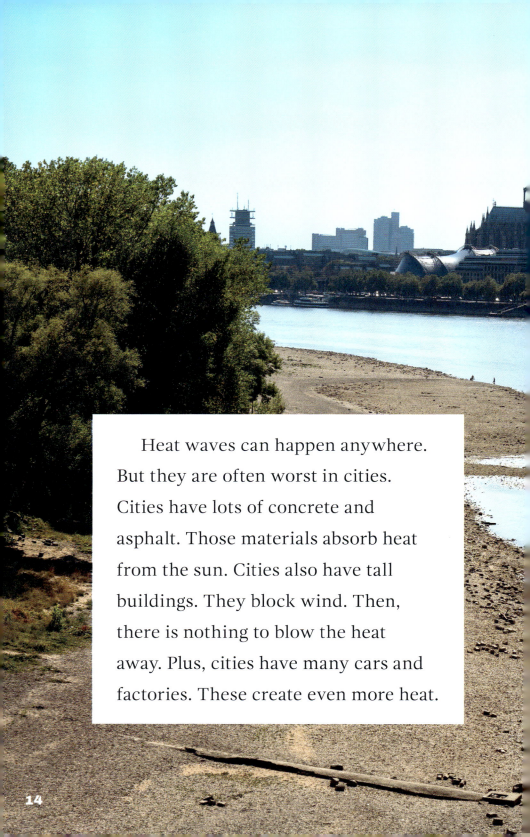

Heat waves can happen anywhere. But they are often worst in cities. Cities have lots of concrete and asphalt. Those materials absorb heat from the sun. Cities also have tall buildings. They block wind. Then, there is nothing to blow the heat away. Plus, cities have many cars and factories. These create even more heat.

Heat waves can warm rivers and lakes. That can harm plants and animals in the water.

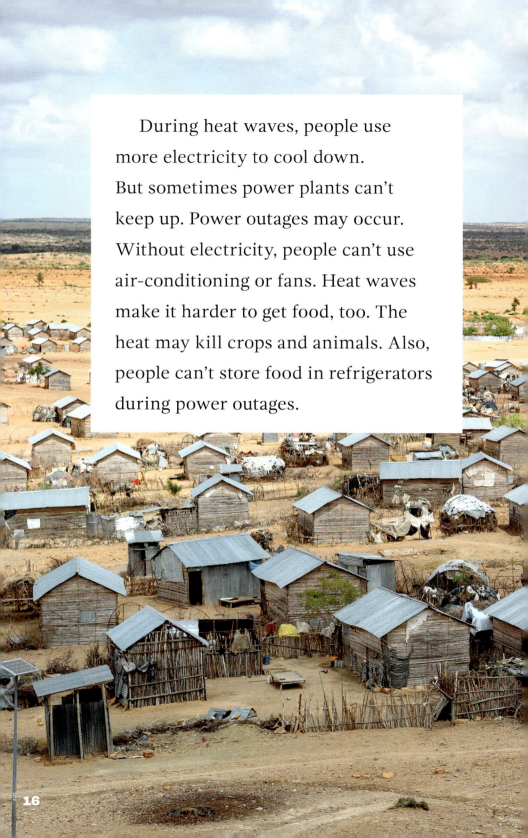

During heat waves, people use more electricity to cool down. But sometimes power plants can't keep up. Power outages may occur. Without electricity, people can't use air-conditioning or fans. Heat waves make it harder to get food, too. The heat may kill crops and animals. Also, people can't store food in refrigerators during power outages.

MORE PROBLEMS

Heat waves tend to cause the most harm in areas that are already struggling. For example, Bangladesh saw food shortages in the early 2020s. The country also faced environmental disasters. Then, heat waves added even more problems.

Since 2016, droughts and heat waves have hit Somalia. They have caused many people to leave their homes.

Often, older people cannot sweat as well as younger people.

Extreme heat can lead to health problems. Heat stress and heatstroke are two examples. These problems happen when the body cannot cool itself. Heat stress can cause harm to organs. Heatstroke occurs when a person does not sweat enough to cool off. Extreme sun exposure or dehydration can cause heatstroke.

YOUNG AND OLD

Each year, 500,000 people die from heat. Many are people who are very young or very old. Their bodies are not as good at cooling down.

Chapter 3

HEAT WAVE HISTORY

In the early 1900s, scientists started using math to predict weather. However, the math was very complicated. So, it took a long time to make forecasts.

Scientist Vilhelm Bjerknes was one of the first people to use math to predict weather.

In the mid-1900s, scientists started using computers. That made calculations faster. Scientists also spent more time studying long-term patterns. They learned more about the climate. They began making predictions further into the future.

1936 HEAT WAVE

A heat wave struck the United States in 1936. Many places saw extreme heat. In Illinois, temperatures passed 100 degrees Fahrenheit (38°C) for 12 straight days. About 5,000 people across the country died from the heat.

In the 1930s, the Dust Bowl caused droughts and killed crops. The 1936 heat wave was part of it.

Scientists completed the EDSAC computer in 1947. It began making weather forecasts in 1952.

Scientists studied the atmosphere. They also studied the ocean. Computers helped predict how they would behave. Scientists first simulated the atmosphere in the 1950s. They made models to predict seasonal patterns.

In 1969, scientists took the next step. They made an even more complicated model. It simulated both the atmosphere and the ocean. The model showed how they affected each other.

In 2011, a new branch of climate science formed. It was called attribution research. The new field focused on extreme weather events. Scientists studied how climate change affects these events. They realized the events were becoming more common.

Between the 1960s and 2020s, the number of heat waves in the United States tripled.

LOOKING BACK

Some scientists also looked to the past. They studied the history of climate change. Scientists looked back millions of years. That helped them understand more about the current and future climate.

HELPING PAKISTAN

In 2022 and 2023, droughts and floods caused major harm to Pakistan. Food prices went up. Many people struggled. But the problems didn't end there. Scientists predicted that severe heat waves would hit in 2024.

Aid groups put together emergency response teams. When the heat waves hit, many Pakistanis struggled. But the response teams were ready to help. They provided health services. They provided water and shelter, too. The early forecasts saved lives.

In Pakistan, volunteers passed out water to help people stay hydrated.

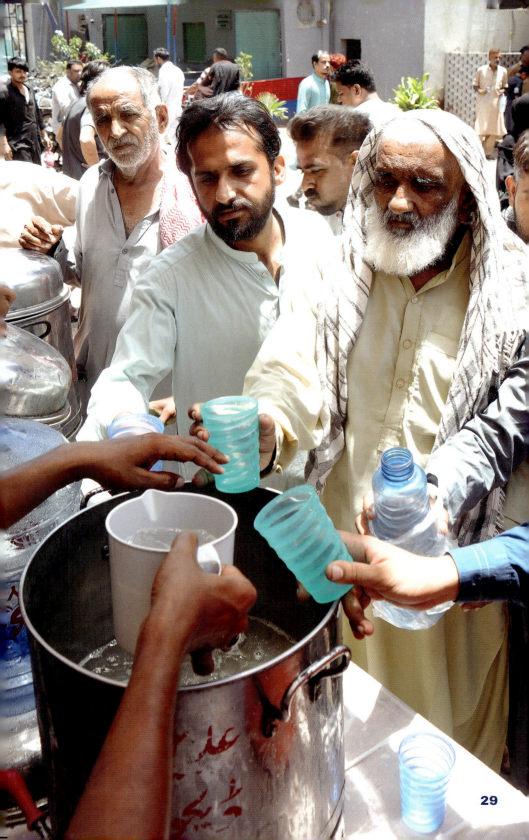

Chapter 4

FORECASTING HEAT

Today, heat wave forecasts use several types of models. Some models make short-term predictions. These are called weather models.

Many news channels share weather forecasts.

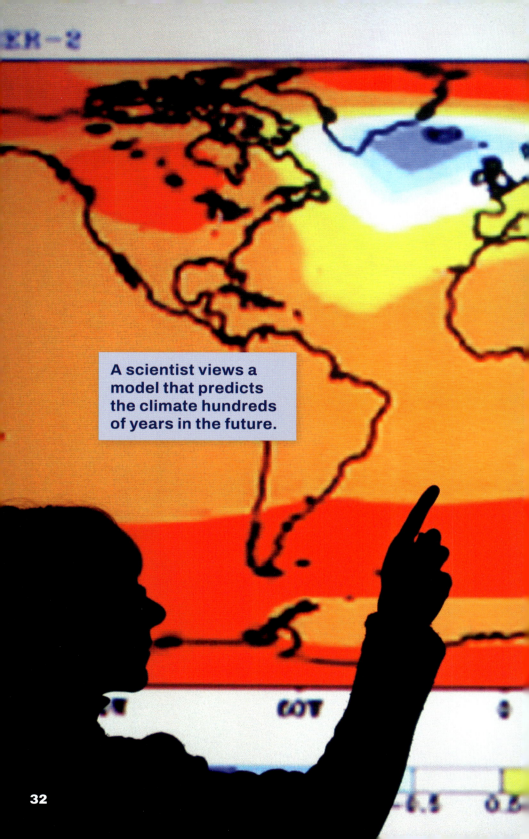

A scientist views a model that predicts the climate hundreds of years in the future.

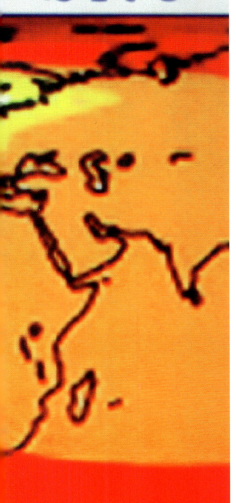

Other models make long-term forecasts. These are called climate models. They predict the climate over decades or centuries. Some models look even further into the future. Scientists try to find out how the climate will affect heat. Their studies show that heat waves may be much stronger in the future.

SEASONAL SCALES

Some models fit between weather and climate models. The models look a few weeks or months in the future. They are called seasonal and sub-seasonal models. These models often help officials prepare for coming heat seasons.

Scientists also try to figure out where heat waves will be strongest. Simple sensors can measure heat and humidity in the air. That helps scientists find heat islands. These are areas that tend to get hotter than other places nearby.

Temperatures in New York City can be more than 9 degrees Fahrenheit (5°C) warmer than nearby areas.

HOT SPOTS

In 2012 and 2013, scientists put 150 sensors in Madison, Wisconsin. The sensors tracked temperatures and humidity. The sensors worked automatically. They took measurements every 15 minutes. Scientists found that the densest areas got the hottest.

NASA has launched many weather satellites into space.

Scientists also study how hot certain surfaces get. They use sensors on satellites and airplanes. Then, they measure large areas. Airplanes can take more detailed measurements than satellites can. But planes are more expensive to use. Satellites can track larger areas. But they don't offer as much detail.

YEAR TO YEAR

Scientists in Arizona used satellites to study heat. The scientists looked at different parts of Phoenix. They took measurements for several years. The scientists noticed changes. Some areas had many new roads and buildings. These areas heated up more than other areas.

Scientists use measurements and data to make risk maps. These maps show places where heat waves might strike. Short-term maps look at upcoming days and weeks. Long-term maps show places that will be affected further into the future.

Wildfires often start in hot, dry areas. Places with heat waves can be at high risk of wildfires.

Chapter 5

STAYING SAFE

Public health workers and weather scientists work together. They learn how much heat is dangerous to human health. That way, officials know when to warn people.

When temperatures reach 103 degrees Fahrenheit (39°C), many people start having heat-related illnesses.

People can receive heat warnings on their phones.

Scientists and officials send out alerts. They may send out heat watches. These alerts mean severe heat is possible. Heat watches do not mean a heat wave is certain. But they tell people to pay close attention to forecasts. Heat warnings are another type of alert. They tell people a heat wave is expected in the next day or two.

RECORD HEAT

In 2024, a heat wave struck the United States for days. Across the country, scientists measured record temperatures. About 120 million people were placed under heat warnings.

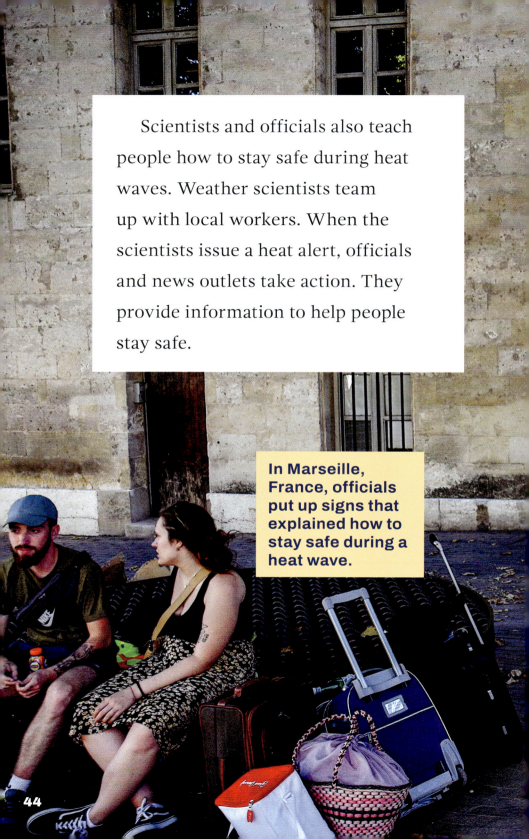

Scientists and officials also teach people how to stay safe during heat waves. Weather scientists team up with local workers. When the scientists issue a heat alert, officials and news outlets take action. They provide information to help people stay safe.

In Marseille, France, officials put up signs that explained how to stay safe during a heat wave.

CANICULES
FORTES CHALEURS

Connaissez-vous les bons gestes pour vous protéger ?

Je demande des nouvelles à ma famille, mes amis...

Je ne fais pas d'effort ou de sport trop fatiguant

Je bois beaucoup d'eau

Je ne sors pas aux heures les plus chaudes

Je ne reste pas en plein soleil (je cherche l'ombre)

Je ne bois pas d'alcool

Je ferme les volets pendant la journée

Je passe plusieurs heures dans un endroit frais ou climatisé (musée, cinéma...)

En cas de malaise, contactez immédiatement les secours.

URGENCE 114
par sms ou fax pour personnes sourdes ou malentendantes

Ou faites appeler le **15**

Retrouvez tous les bons gestes pour vous protéger sur marseille.fr

45

Santé publique
France

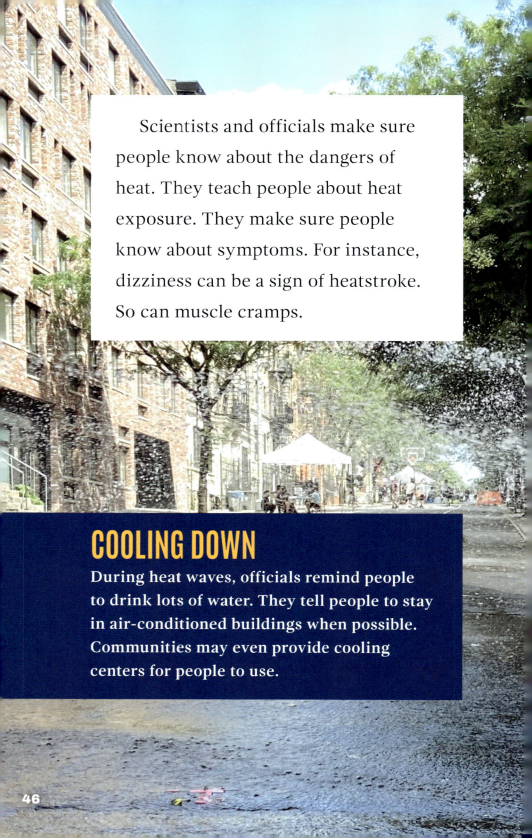

Scientists and officials make sure people know about the dangers of heat. They teach people about heat exposure. They make sure people know about symptoms. For instance, dizziness can be a sign of heatstroke. So can muscle cramps.

COOLING DOWN

During heat waves, officials remind people to drink lots of water. They tell people to stay in air-conditioned buildings when possible. Communities may even provide cooling centers for people to use.

In some cities, officials open up fire hydrants. People can cool off in the water.

SAVING LIVES

In 1995, a heat wave hit Chicago, Illinois. More than 700 people died. So, officials and scientists took action. They wanted to make sure they were prepared for extreme heat in the future. They hoped to provide better treatment and responses.

In 1999, another heat wave struck Chicago. Public health workers were ready. They warned people across the city. They quickly treated people in need. Temperatures were similar to the 1995 heat wave. But this time, only 100 people died. The preparation saved lives.

Many people in Chicago went to cooling centers to get out of the heat.

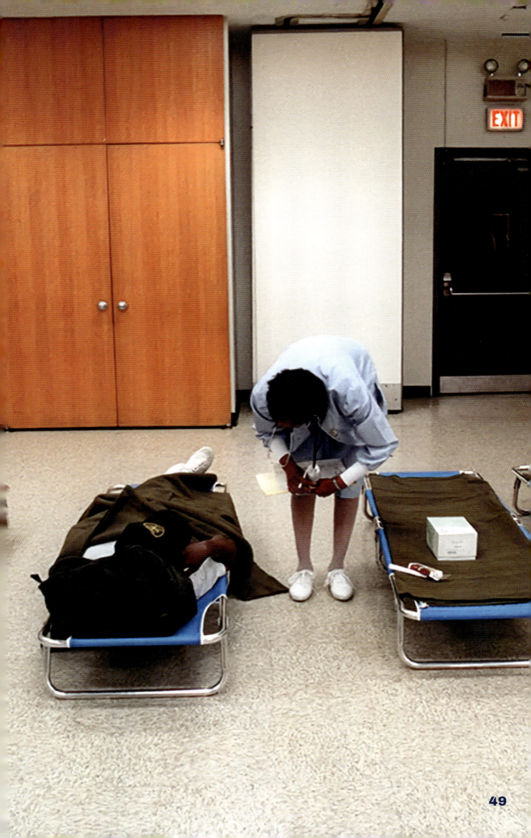

During heat waves, groups may offer water and food in low-income neighborhoods.

Chapter 6

PREVENT AND PREPARE

Scientists and officials prepare long before heat waves strike. They find ways to reduce extreme heat. They hope to make future heat waves less harmful.

Heat waves are usually most dangerous in cities. So, officials think about heat waves when planning for city growth. Cars increase heat. For that reason, officials may plan walkable neighborhoods. That way, people don't have to use cars as much. Officials also add more vegetation. Grasses and trees remove heat from the air. The plants provide shade, too.

COOL PAVEMENTS

Concrete and asphalt take in lots of heat during the day. Then the heat is released at night. So, some cities are building smaller roads. They're planting trees for shade, too. Scientists are also working to create cooler paving materials. These materials may reflect sunlight instead of soaking it up.

Cities can provide trains or buses for people to take instead of cars.

The air above green roofs can be 7 degrees Fahrenheit (4°C) cooler than the air above normal roofs.

Green roofs and rooftop gardens help with heat, too. Surface temperatures on green roofs are much lower than on regular roofs. Some green roofs have a thin layer of plants. These plants don't need much care. Other green roofs have large plants and trees. They may look like a garden or park. But they are more expensive to care for.

COOL ROOFS

Some buildings have "cool roofs." These roofs use reflective materials. Cool roofs transfer less heat from the sun into the building. They also let go of heat more quickly.

Scientists and officials are also trying to deal with climate change. Decreasing the use of fossil fuels is one major way to help. Governments may create laws that companies must follow. Laws can force power plants to be cleaner, too. Officials may also prepare for extreme weather. For example, they may build cooling centers.

CLIMATE CHANGE

Heat waves are most harmful in places where the climate has changed the most. Africa's Sahel region is one of these areas. There, temperatures are rising 1.5 times faster than in other parts of the world. Heat kills plants and causes droughts. In Central Sahel, 7.5 million people did not have enough food in 2024.

Cooling centers are often at libraries, government buildings, and community centers.